The Problems With Men

By
Jo Ann Bullard

Copyright © 2012
ISBN- 0615873839
All Rights Reserved
Published 2013

For more information contact:
Jo Ann Bullard
JA2Bullard@gmail.com

Lyrics and Books From the Heart Publishing Company, Inc.
Knoxville, Tennessee

This book is dedicated to women and written from a woman's point of view. Each poem deals with the trials, tribulations, and joys of being a woman. Only a woman can understand the problems they have with men. However, each woman also understands the uniqueness and pride of being a woman.

Table of Contents

The Problems With Men

The problems with men are they never apologize
They never seem to compromise
They always seem to patronize
They always seem to rationalize

They never hear what you say
They always want their own way
They never care about the cost
They always want to be boss

They never seem to take the blame
They always want their game
They never care what hurts you
They always want to do what they do

They never seem to see your side
They always want their ride
They never care about a fight
They always want you at night

Sometimes we women wonder why we try
To deal with men but we know why
You see, we know it takes a man
To make a woman feel like a woman

All I Want is For You to Love Me

I can buy what I ain't got
I can buy a house with a lot
What I want can't be bought with money
All I want is for you to love me

I don't want a fancy ring
While you go out on a fling
I don't want no fancy home
While I'm waiting for you alone

I don't want a fancy car
While I'm wondering where you are
I don't want no fancy flight
While I'm waiting for you at night

I don't want no fancy financial plan
While I know you're with another woman
I don't want no fancy holiday
While I'm praying for you to stay

That fancy ring will grow old
That fancy car will grow cold
All I want can't be bought with money
All I want is for you to love me

Men Think Below the Belt

When a man sees a beautiful woman pass
He thinks of her behind and a whiskey glass
He starts thinking below the waist
His brain seems to turn to paste

When he remembers the books he's read
Everything but sex goes out of his head
His mind can't compete with his fire
His brain can't control the rise of his desire

His brain and mind go out the door
He's fantasizing about sex with her on the floor
There's only one thing he wants to do
Make love to her body until he's through

As his lust grows for her body
He's not interested in thinking or reality
There's only one thing on his mind
Feeling her body from front to behind

Throughout history, it's been the same
Men are just men and not to blame
We women enjoy seeing men melt
When they're thinking below the belt

If You Don't, I'll Have to Go

I'm standing at the door
I don't want to fight anymore
There's nothing left for you to say
Except that I want you to stay

Please don't start looking sad
Please don't yell at me looking mad
All I want to see and hear
Are words that mean you care

Honey, I'm tired of the game
Of pointing the finger of blame
I'm sick of all these fears
And the heartache of these years

I knew it would come to the day
When I felt I had to go away
Baby, tell me something I'll believe
I don't want to have to leave

Say something I can understand
Touch me tenderly with your hand
Tell me something I want to know
If you don't, I'll have to go

Hold me as you never did before
Keep me from walking out the door
Show me what I need to know
Baby, I don't want to have to go

I'll Give My Love to You For Free

I can't even touch a star
I can't reach that far
I can't find a money tree
I'll give my love to you for free

I'll give you what I own
I'll give you my fancy home
I'll give you a bedroom key
I'll give my love to you for free

I'll give you a big fancy house
I'll give you a computer with a mouse
I'll give you all my money
I'll give my love to you for free

I'll give you the world on a string
I'll give you a big diamond ring
I'll give you a farm with a tree
I'll give my love to you for free

I can't seem to catch the wind
I can't change what's already been
All I have to give you is me
I'll give my love to you for free

What A Woman Knows

Men may think they know, but they're blind
To a woman's feelings and a woman's mind
They may try to catch the wind that blows
But they won't know what a woman knows

A woman knows what it's like to try
A woman knows what it's like to cry
A woman knows the feeling of trying in vain
A woman knows the pain of crying in pain

A woman knows what it's like to live
A woman knows what it's like to give
A woman knows what it's like to live alone
A woman knows what it's like when it's gone

A woman knows what it's like to be used
A woman knows what it's like to be abused
A woman knows what it's like to be used selfishly
A woman knows what it's like to be abused needlessly

A woman knows what it's like to have no respect
A woman knows what it's like to just get neglect
A woman knows what it's like to feel disrespected
A woman knows what it's like to feel neglected

Men may think they can control everything
In the land of to thee I sing
They can't catch the wind that blows
They'll never know what a woman knows

I'll See You Tomorrow

I'm not going to do this anymore
I said as he walked out the door
But I know the words were not true
I'd dream of the next moment with you

Sometimes the night's just too long
And the pain is just too strong
And you need someone to hold you in the night
And you don't care if it's wrong or right

They say the soul is willing, but the flesh is weak
And we don't mean the words we speak
Love don't always let us understand
And it's not stopped by a wedding band

Fish gotta swim, and birds gotta fly
Some gotta laugh, and some gotta cry
I'll take what love with you I can borrow
I don't want to, but I'll see you tomorrow

Blue Song

Sometimes friends just aren't around
Sometimes love just can't be found
Sometimes peace just can't be had
Sometimes all I feel is sad

I've got those old blues today
I don't even know how to say
The words to tell you all about
The feelings that I need to get out

I've forgotten how to tell what's real
In all these feelings that I feel
All I know is that it's all the same
Just another person, just another name

I don't even know how I got to this place
Maybe it was just part of the human rat race
Maybe I've just seen too much pain
And maybe I've just felt too much rain

I can only just try to cope
And hold on to the idea of hope
All I know is today seems full of sorrow
Maybe it'll be better tomorrow

Bring Your Cash Home to Me

I don't care about the games you play
I don't care about the words you say
I don't care about the women you see
Bring your cash home to me

I don't care about your drinking
I don't care about your thinking
I don't care about where you may be
Bring your cash home to me

I don't care about your cheating
I don't care about who you're meeting
I don't care about your lame story
Bring your cash home to me

I don't care about your lying
I don't care about your crying
I don't care about your history
Bring your cash home to me

I don't care about where you go
I don't care about who you know
Being a lying and cheating man ain't free
Bring your cash home to me

I used to care in better days
You continued your lying and cheating ways
Though I may listen to your trash
I'm only staying for the cash

I'm His Wife

The phone rang, and I knew
It was the other woman calling about you
She said, "I know you're his wife
I'm the other woman in his life"

Both of us are going to lose
It's not like him to choose
All he wants is just to play
He doesn't love us anyway

Both of us are gonna cry
It's just like him to lie
All he wants is us to play his game
He doesn't think that he's to blame

Both of us knew he's unfair
It's not like him to care
He wants to have his cake and eat it too
He doesn't care about me or you

Both of us are gonna pay
It's not like him to stay
All he wants is a wine and a song
He doesn't care if it's wrong

I listened, and then I said
You're like the books I've already read
You may be the other woman in his life
But I've got him, and I'm his wife

Men Are Like Little Boys

Men are like little boys
When it comes to their toys
Whether it is a fishing boat or hunting knife
They like them better than their wife

They gotta have their pick-up truck
To go out with the boys and leave you stuck
They want that fancy I-phone
To make a date and leave you home

They gotta have their favorite gun
To go hunting before the work is done
They want their fancy four-by-four
To leave you alone waiting by the door

Men can have all their toys
Men can act like little boys
Whether it is a fishing boat or hunting knife
Nothing is better than their wife

Your toys can't give you what a woman can
When she makes you feel like a man
You know your woman has her way
Of making you put your toys away

Your Honey Do List

Honey, please put the toilet seat down
Please don't leave your trash laying around
I don't want to fight about this
Here's your honey do list

There are things you can do
Why do I have to make a list for you?
It doesn't seem to matter to you anyway
You don't seem to hear a word I say

We've gone thru this before
You get mad and walk out the door
It always turns out the same
I'm wrong and the one to blame

I want more, and I want better
We're both in this together
I'm sure that this is fair
It's time for you to do your share

Honey, please take the trash out
I won't beg, and I won't shout
I'm tired of fighting about this
Here's your honey do list

I Ain't No Alice In Wonderland

I ain't no Alice in Wonderland
I ain't no one night stand
If you think you'll milk the cow for free
Better not even talk to me

I don't care about your cash
I won't listen to your trash
I'm not here for your joy
I won't be your little toy

I won't put up with your neglect
I won't put up with your disrespect
I won't put up with games you play
I won't put up with lies you say

I won't ignore your whiskey glass
I won't pretend to be second class
I won't allow you to make me mad
I won't allow you to make me sad

I've known your kind before
I'm not going to take it anymore
One thing you should understand
I ain't no Alice In Wonderland

When Good Love Goes Bad

There is something I've got to do
And I need to talk to you
But I can't find the words to say
That I'm leaving you today

Honey, let me hold your hand
And I hope that you'll understand
I can't stay with you anymore
And it's not like it was before

There is something I want you to know
And I hope that you let me go
I can't love you like I should
And I can't stay even if I could

Let me hold you and wipe away the tears
And I'll always remember all these years
But I've got to go, and it's so sad
When times change, and good love goes bad

So it's time for both of us to see
And what will be will always be
There's nothing left to do, nothing left to say
When good love is only a memory of yesterday

Once is Only A lost Love's Lament

Once I shared a beautiful dream
Now all I want to do is scream
Once I had a love that was heaven sent
Now once is only a lost love's lament

Once I prayed to the heavens above
Please send me someone to love
Once my prayers were answered and came true
When they sent me our love and you

Once I shouted on the mountain
About the warm waters of love's fountain
Once I wished upon a star in the night
That our love would work out right

Once I bragged to the clear blue sea
That you would stay with me
Once I talked to a waterfall
About how you and I had it all

The sky cried, the mountain started to roar
My time with you and love were no more
Once was only a time that's been
Once with you will never come again

I Like What He Does At Night

I like the way he wiggles his hips
I like the way he uses his lips
I may not believe a word he said
I like what he does in bed

He may not be a superstar
He may not drive a fancy car
I may not like what I see
I like the way he is with me

I may not like the friends he meets
I like what he does under the sheets
He may not even try to understand
I like what he does with his hand

He may not care about my mind
I like the way he takes his sweet time
He may not even have a lot
I like the way he uses what he's got

He always seems to do it in a way
That makes me want more every day
Though things might not seem right
I like what he does at night

A Woman's Work is Never Done

I don't know what a man is thinking
When he goes out with his friends drinking
Getting up with the morning sun
A woman's work is never done

It seems a man never knows
Just how many places a woman goes
It seems a man never cares
About how many hats a woman wears

A woman gets the kids ready for school
A woman takes the kids to the pool
A woman makes sure the homework's right
A woman cooks the meals at night

A man seems to think when he gets home
The woman has to do all the work alone
Even though there's a lot he could do
He's done his work, and he's through

When it's time for a woman to rest
A man will be ready and at his best
All he wants is sex and his fun
A woman's work is never done

A Message to All the Men

I've got a message to all the men
Don't treat a woman as a second class citizen
You better treat them better than before
They're not going to take it anymore

Women want their equal pay
Women want their equal say
They're going to take it, like it or not
Women want more than what they've got

Some of you men may cheat and lie
Some of you men may make your woman cry
Some of you men are being bad
Some of you men are making your woman sad

Better think about what you're doing
It's yourself that you're fooling
Wake up before it's too late
She's your partner, not just your mate

Men better be tender and kind
Be aware of the new woman's mind
Things are not done as they were done
It's a brand new day with a brand new sun

If Teardrops Were Made of Gold

I can't remember all the times I've cried
I can't count all the times I've tried
I can't count the lies I've been told
If teardrops were made of gold

I've cried so many tears over you
I can't even talk about what I've been through
I don't know why I continue to stay
I don't even know what to say

I don't even try to understand
Why I love that cheating, lying man
I don't even know how or why
I love that man that makes me cry

I don't know why when we fight
I cry myself to sleep at night
I don't know why I'm in pain
I love a man that drives me insane

Must be a power that I can't see
Must be stronger than I can be
I'd be a rich woman from all the tears I hold
If teardrops were made of gold

Honey, You Can't Treat Me This A Way

Come on in and close the door
I've been waiting and pacing the floor
Sit down and listen to what I say
Honey, you can't treat me this a way

I've got to take care of myself
I may not have that much left
I'm tired of the games you play
Honey, you can't treat me this a way

You want me to forgive and forget
I've still got my self respect
What you do to me is not okay
Honey, you can't treat me this a way

It seems that every time we have a fight
I'm always wrong, and you're always right
We're as different as night and day
Honey, you can't treat me this a way

Honey, you've hurt me many times before
I'm not gonna take it anymore
It's up to you what you do today
Honey, you can't treat me this a way

I will forgive, but not forget
You can't take my self respect
I hope you hear what I have to say
Honey, you can't treat me this a way

Love's Gotta A Hold On Me

I've been thinking and trying to find
A reason why I don't leave you behind
I guess the only thing it could be
Love's gotta a hold on me

You've given me every reason to walk away
I just don't know why I stay
Even though I long to be free
Love's gotta a hold on me

I feel like I can't do it anymore
I even try to walk out the door
Something stops me when I try to flee
Love's gotta a hold on me

It doesn't seem to matter what you do
I can't see myself living without you
I feel like a possum up a tree
Love's gotta a hold on me

I know that this feeling is real
I know how you make me feel
I'll tell all about love's power and glory
Love's gotta a hold on me

Somehow

Go on out the door
I can't take it anymore
I don't want to cry
Somehow I'll get by

Somehow I'll make it thru
Somehow I'll get over you
Somehow I'll find a way
Somehow I'll see another day

Somehow I'll find a friend
Somehow I'll forget what's been
Somehow I'll fight my tears
Somehow I'll face my fears

Somehow I'll sleep at night
Somehow I'll win the fight
Somehow I'll accept you're gone
Somehow I'll do it alone

Somehow I'll get thru the sorrow
Somehow I'll get to tomorrow
Somehow I'll find a way to get thru
Somehow I'll find a way to forget about you

Still Going to Love You Tomorrow

There's some words that I can't say
There's some games that I can't play
There's some things that I can't do
There's some times that I never knew

I can't find the right words to say
How much that I miss you when you're away
I can't tell you when I'll write you a song
Because the words seem to come out wrong

I can't seem to find a way
To play the games that people play
I can't play because it's just too real
For me to play about what I feel

I don't know what I'm going to do
When it comes to my love for you
I don't know why it feels so right
Even though I'm lonely at night

I don't know if I ever knew
What the price was for loving you
I don't know if I can take the sorrow
But I'm still going to love you tomorrow

In Two Worlds

Baby, I don't want to have to go
Baby, I'm just trying to let you know
That these two faces that I see
Are in two worlds, and it's killing me

You keep telling me that you care
But I look around, and you're not there
Seems all we do these days is fight
Each one thinking they're right

I keep feeling so all alone
One minute here, next minute gone
Both of us keep wanting it our way
And neither of us know what to say

We keep pretending that it's right
Wish we may, wish we might
Both of us know in our heart
That we live in two worlds apart

But both of us keep holding on
To a world that we've both known
But time moves on, no one's to blame
These two worlds will never be the same

It's Just Too Much of a Price to Pay

I get more pleasure from the chocolate and dove
Than I get from your so called love
Being with you and the games you play
It's just too much of a price to pay

You seem to think I can't live without you
And you can do what you want to do
But you forget one thing for sure
I lived without you around before

You said that I don't have a right to speak
And you may think that I'm weak
You seem to think I can't get along
But you forget that I'm strong

You think that you can disrespect me
And you may believe that I can't see
You seem to think I have nothing left
But you forget I have myself

You may think that I can't make it alone
And I'll fall apart when you're gone
If being with you costs myself to play
It's just too much of a price to pay

They're Not the Only Cars on the Road

I think men need to be told
They're not the only cars on the road
They're not always in the driver's seat
Sometimes they're on a two way street

The road doesn't always run one way
Sometimes there's a toll to pay
Men can be wrong and lost
Sometimes they have to pay the cost

Men would stop the car and fight
Before they would admit they weren't right
Men seem to think they own the lane
And have every right to cause you pain

Men don't even know how to brake
When they come to give and take
Men seem to put on the speed
And run from you if you're in need

Men need to try and understand
They're women and men drivers in the land
And I don't care what they've been told
They're not the only cars on the road

Just Say Something Nice to Me

Sometimes two people may have a fight
Doesn't matter who's wrong or right
Sometimes two people may disagree
Just say something nice to me

Don't turn and walk away
When I have something to say
Don't tell me just let me be
Just say something nice to me

Don't tell me to forgive and forget
When you know I need respect
Don't tell me you can't see
Just say something nice to me

Don't pretend you don't hear
When I need someone to care
Don't tell me about our history
Just say something nice to me

Just tell me this is real
Show me you care how I feel
Show me something I want to see
Just say something nice to me

A Woman's Right

I think it's time to talk to you
I'm tired of the things you do
What I say will cause a fight
I'm gonna tell you about a woman's right

A woman has a right to respect
Don't expect me to forgive and forget
A woman has a right to be heard
Don't pretend you don't hear a word

A woman has a right to tenderness
Don't expect me to take anything less
A woman has a right to her say
Don't expect me to let you have your way

A woman has a right to speak
Don't expect me to turn the other cheek
A woman has a right to equality
Don't pretend that you can't see

I'm a woman, and I'm proud of myself
Don't think that I don't have anything left
I'm giving you a chance, though we might fight
You're gonna give me a woman's right

We Love Them Anyway

I don't know why we even try
To talk to men who make us cry
I guess it's the way it's always been
The problems for women are men

They always want to have their way
They never listen to anything you say
They don't give you any respect
They always want you to forgive and forget

They never seem to care
They never seem to hear
They never seem to compromise
They never see to apologize

They're always playing their game
They're always saying you're to blame
They always make you mad
They always leave you sad

Men have problems that make us cry
Most of us don't know why we try
We know about the games men play
But we know we love them anyway

Saying I'm Sorry is Not Enough

Sometimes the same song grows old
Sometimes the warm love grows cold
Sometimes life's hard and is just too tough
Sometimes saying I'm sorry is not enough

You know I wish I could
Go back to a place when times were good
I can't change the times that's been
I don't want to hear I'm sorry again

I don't know what's the matter with you
Why you think you can do what you want to do
You know I wished it hadn't come to the day
When I know I can't believe a word you say

I can't pretend when it's always the same
You never believe you're the one to blame
I can't help it, but I'm not that strong
To always hear how I'm the one always wrong

This same song has grown old
This warm love has grown cold
This road has grown too tough
This time saying I'm sorry is not enough

I'm Thru

I don't seem to matter to you
It's so sad, but it's true
If that's the way it's gonna be
Then hit the door, forget about me

It don't seem to matter in your mind
You pretend to have eyes that are blind
It don't seem to matter how much I care
You pretend to have ears that can't hear

Time and time again, I talk in vain
About the times you bring me pain
Day after day, you make me cry
Then you pretend to not know why

I'm not your puppet on a string
I can't forget about myself and everything
Saying you're sorry ain't enough anymore
Think it's time you should hit the door

And maybe I want what ain't gonna be
I still gotta think and care about me
And maybe I don't matter to you
But I matter to me, and I'm thru

And Where Are You

Sun's up, and the temperature's hot
Sometimes you're up, sometimes you're not
Just sitting, thinking about what to do
By myself, and where are you?

I don't have to go to work today
I'd like to go out and play
I'd like to go do something new
Got time off, and where are you?

Times a passing, and I'm getting older
Pretty soon it'll start getting colder
Guess it's time to see what's true
Clock's a ticking, and where are you?

Words won't change what I have to see
Time to take a dose of reality
And asking where are you in my life
Doesn't change the fact you're with your wife

Today I may be blue
Today I may feel like a fool
Today I know where you're gonna be
But tomorrow, you'll be with me

No Matter

You can run, and you can hide
You can have your wife by your side
You can try and shut me out
But I'm someone that you care about

You can say what you have to say
You can even try to stay away
You can do what you have to do
You can even believe that it's not true

You can go and play your role
You can even pretend that you don't know
You can run and try to flee
You can even try to forget about me

You know no matter what you do
You can't run away from that part of you
That loves me and you know
That love will be wherever you go

No matter what you try to say
No matter how you try to play
No matter what you try to be
No matter, you're still in love with me

Love's Fool

I guess I'll go check the door
Smoke a cigarette and pace the floor
Maybe I was wrong, maybe I was right
Guess I'll have another sleepless night

I don't know why love does you this way
Don't know what to do, don't know what to say
It seems sometimes you don't understand
Why you still love that no good man

You say you can't do this no more
But you can't wait for him to walk thru the door
He'll tell you lies you don't even believe
But you'll never be able to tell him to leave

Love just makes a fool out of you
And leaves you not knowing what to do
You ask yourself why do I need him so much
But the answers come in the form of his touch

Love has done made a fool out of me
I guess that's the way it's gonna be
But if that's the cost of being with you
I guess I'll just be love's fool

This is For the One I'll Always Remember

We've all done things that we regret
There's some things we can't forget
I remember making love to you in September
This is for the one I'll always remember

It was a time of the summer's heat
There were times we would meet
Our bodies said all they needed to say
That was a sweet time of yesterday

We dreamed of places we wanted to go
We talked about things only lovers know
We wished upon a star each night
We arose with hope in the morning light

I never had to ever pretend
It was if it had always been
We were planning of me being your wife
We were in the prime of our life

Then one day the heat turned to cold
When you died, and I grew old
But I'll always remember making love in September
This is for the one I'll always remember

I Want Someone to Love Me For Me

I may not know how to sing
I may not have a diamond ring
I may not be what you want me to be
I want someone to love me for me

I may not have a beautiful body
I may not have a lot of money
I may not be a sight to see
I want someone to love me for me

I may not drive a fancy car
I may not be a movie star
I may not have won the lottery
I want someone to love me for me

I may not have a pretty face
I may not live in a fancy place
I may not have a degree in history
I want someone to love me for me

I want someone that I can trust
I want someone who feels more than lust
I want someone whose love is for free
I want someone to love me for me

Go Find Yourself Another Toy

You can't tell me where to walk
You can't tell me when to talk
You can't tell me what to be
You can't tell me who to see

I'll travel where I want to go
I'll know who I want to know
I'll talk when I want to speak
I'll seek what I want to seek

Why does a man think he can control
A woman's mind he'll never know?
Why does a man seem so blind
To the power of a woman's mind?

A woman needs someone to care
A woman needs someone to be there
A woman needs someone to hold her hand
A woman needs someone to understand

I'm more than a puppet on a string
I'm more than a woman with a ring
If you think I exist only for your joy
Go and find yourself another toy

A Woman's Feelings

In the world of the real and unreal
Men don't seem to know how we feel
In the valleys and mountains of the land
Men don't seem to ever understand

Men don't seem to ever know
Why we go places that we go
Men don't seem to care anyway
Why we say the things that we say

It seems that one's talking to someone with no ears
When we talk about all our fears
It seems that one's trying to show the blind
Things to see when we speak our mind

Men don't seem to care about our pain
When we try to talk to them in vain
Men don't seem to even worry
About the times they should be sorry

But a woman's feelings are very real
Men should try to understand how we feel
But a man will never try to understand
A woman's feelings in this land

Honey, I Won't Do It No More

I can't pretend that it's right
That you hurt me and call it a fight
I can't pretend that it's right anymore
When you say honey, I won't do it no more

It doesn't matter what I say
You say it's my fault anyway
It doesn't matter what you do
You say it's me and never you

It doesn't matter what it's about
You say you're wrong, and then you shout
It doesn't matter, it's always the same
You say that I'm always to blame

It doesn't matter what I believe
You say it's over, then you leave
It doesn't matter about the bruises I've had
You say that you just got mad

You seem to think that it's right
To hurt me and call it a fight
It's not right, I ain't gonna take it anymore
Don't tell me honey, I won't do it no more

Promises That You Don't Keep

I'm so tired and sick of trying
I'm sick and tired of crying
I think this mountain is just too steep
Built of promises that you don't keep

I've done everything that I can
To try to live with this man
I can't seem to understand or see
Why you say it's always me

I've said everything I need to say
But you don't seem to hear me anyway
I'm tired of everything being the same
When you say I'm always to blame

I've tried to make you understand
There's more to love than holding my hand
I'm tired of every time we have a fight
That you say you're always right

I didn't know what else to do
To try to make it with you
It's time to make you see
The problem is you and not just me

Me and Little Johnny

Guess I'll hide my black eye again
Go to work and try to pretend
Makeup won't hide the pain
Makeup will run with the rain

I guess I'll say I ran into the door
I've heard all your promises before
I've tried to forgive and forget
I've lost any hint of self respect

This time Little Johnny saw my eye
He looked up and started to cry
Mommy what did Daddy do to you
I knew then what I had to do

I said sometimes Mommy and Daddy fight
Sometimes things just don't work out right
This time me and you just can't stay
Mommy and you are going away

I packed up and walked out the door
Me and Little Johnny can't take it anymore
Sometimes it takes a child's voice
To tell you that you have no choice

Somehow me and Little Johnny will be alright
I won't have to lie and won't have to fight
The pain and wounds are just too deep
From abuse and promises you can't keep

About the Author

Jo Ann Bullard is an author and a devout animal lover. She writes song lyrics and poetry books to support her passion for saving animals. She pays adoption fees for animals in shelters to give them the opportunity to find homes and provide pet adoptions. She believes that one animal who dies needlessly is one animal too many.

www.ingramcontent.com/pod-product-compliance
Lightning Source LLC
Chambersburg PA
CBHW060632030426
42337CB00018B/3327